34

THE WAMPANOAG

KATHERINE M. DOHERTY AND CRAIG A. DOHERTY

THE WAMPANOAG

Franklin Watts   A Division of Grolier Publishing
New York   London   Hong Kong   Sydney   Danbury, Connecticut
A First Book

To our families

Cover photograph copyright © Ben Klaffke

Photographs copyright ©: Ben Klaffke: pp. 3, 10, 26, 29, 33, 35, 42, 43, 45, 46, 47, 49, 53, 55, 56; North Wind Picture Archives: pp. 14, 18, 22, 25, 31, 37, 39, 41; FPG International Corp.: pp. 16, 17; The Bettmann Archive: pp. 19, 51; Globe Pequot Press: p. 38.

Library of Congress Cataloging-in-Publication Data
Doherty, Katherine M.
The Wampanoag / by Katherine M. Doherty and Craig A. Doherty.
p. cm. — (A First book)
Includes bibliographical references and index.
ISBN 0-531-20208-9
1. Wampanoag Indians—History—Juvenile literature. 2. Wampanoag Indians—Social life and customs—Juvenile literature. I. Doherty, Craig A. II. Title. III. Series.
E99.W2D65 1995
974.4'004973—dc20   95-18589 CIP
                                                                AC

CONTENTS

EARLY HISTORY

All Native North American nations cherish their beliefs about their origin and the journey of their ancestors to the continent. In the scientific community, however, a commonly held theory proposes that all Native North Americans originally came from Asia. It is believed that some time during the last *Ice Age*, fifteen to forty thousand years ago, hunters crossed the shallow Bering Sea, between Asia and North America, in search of big game. Over thousands of years, this migration extended throughout North, South, and Central America.

In time, the glaciers receded and the climate became milder. The big-game hunters learned to adapt to the new environments in which they lived. Where game and wild edible plants were plentiful, people remained *nomadic*. Others learned how to cultivate plants for food and settled in permanent communities. Some regions, where the soil and climate were good and the game plentiful, were home to both hunter-gatherers and farmers. Hunter-gatherers revisited food sources and followed seasonal animal migrations, while farmers grew their own food. When Europeans began arriving in the late fifteenth century, there were about four hundred separate native nations established throughout the territory later to become the United States.

A COASTAL PEOPLE

For thousands of years the Wampanoag (pronounced wam-puh-NO-ag) have lived in present-day southeastern Massachusetts, including the islands of Martha's Vineyard and Nantucket, and eastern Rhode Island. They are part of a large group of tribes known as Eastern Woodland Indians.

The Wampanoag language is part of the *Algonquian language* family. Their specific dialect is called Massachuset—the name of one of three closely related tribal groups that, with the Wampanoag, formed an alliance. The Massachuset language was also spoken by the Massachuset and Pawtucket tribes.

The name *Wampanoag* appears to have been used first by the Dutch trader Adrian Block in the

THE WAMPANOAG HAVE LIVED IN THE COASTAL REGIONS
OF MASSACHUSETTS FOR THOUSANDS OF YEARS.

early seventeenth century. He referred to the American Indians of the area as Wampanoo—eastern or coastal people. Eventually Wampanaog became the most commonly accepted name for all the tribes in this cultural group.

From earliest times the Wampanoag have lived in the forests of eastern North America. They depended on those forests for their needs. It is estimated that the earliest trace of Native Americans in what is now the northeastern part of the United States is twelve thousand years old. These early people hunted, fished, and searched for their food.

Ancestors of the Wampanoag settled in the area of Cape Cod and the islands off the coast of Massachusetts. They learned to fish and gather a variety of seafood. Then, about three thousand years ago, they became skilled in agriculture, or farming. The development of corn as a crop had slowly made its way north from central Mexico and spread rapidly among native tribes.

The addition of agriculture to the lives of the Wampanoag made it possible for them to build semi-permanent settlements in river valleys. The land along rivers was easier to clear and the soil was better for growing crops.

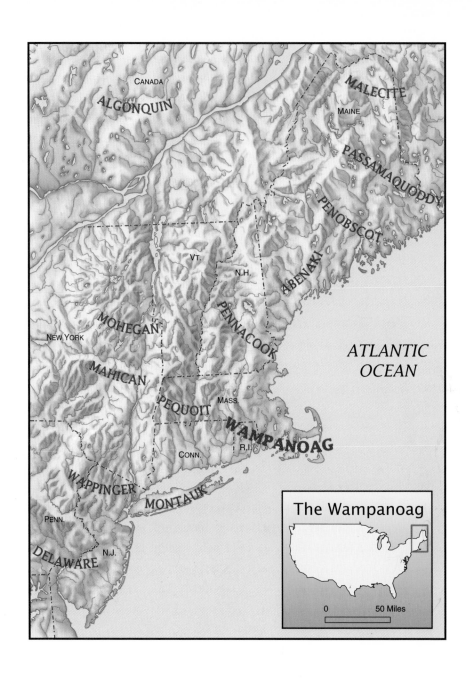

CANADA

ALGONQUIN

MALECITE

MAINE

PASSAMAQUODDY

PENOBSCOT

VT.

N.H.

ABENAKI

MOHEGAN

NEW YORK

PENNACOOK

ATLANTIC
OCEAN

MAHICAN

PEQUOIT

MASS.

WAMPANOAG

CONN.

R.I.

WAPPINGER

MONTAUK

PENN.

DELAWARE

N.J.

The Wampanoag

0   50 Miles

SURVIVING WAR AND ILLNESS

Contact with Europeans grew in the sixteenth century when explorers, fishermen, and traders from Europe began to explore the northeastern coast of North America. One of the first Europeans to explore this area was Giovanni da Verrazano in 1524. At that time, there were between twenty and twenty-five thousand Wampanoags living in this coastal region.

The very earliest Europeans who visited this part of the Americas did not stay. However, they left behind diseases against which American Indians had no resistance. When the English landed at Plymouth in 1620 they did not immediately find any American Indians. The closely related Pawtucket Indians who had lived in the area had been all but wiped out by

BEFORE THE LANDING OF THE ENGLISH AT PLYMOUTH,
A DEADLY DISEASE KILLED A GREAT MANY WAMPANOAG.

European diseases. The few survivors had left the area and moved in with the nearby Wampanoag.

The leader of one Wampanoag community known as the Pokanoket was a man called Massasoit. When the English arrived in 1620, Massasoit was able to communicate with them with the help of Squanto, a leader from the Pawtucket band, who had been kidnapped and taken to Europe where he learned to speak English.

During the first winter of 1620, more than half of the English died. In the spring of 1621, Massasoit made a peace treaty with the governor of the colony, John Carver. This treaty stated that the English would respect the rights of the Pokanoket and, in return, the Pokanoket would not harm the English.

That spring, the settlers planted many crops in their fields. Many of the European crops did not do well. However, the Indian corn flourished. Governor Carver died before the first harvest and William Bradford became the new governor. After the harvest he organized a feast and invited the Wampanoag to the three-day harvest feast of thanksgiving. After that first Thanksgiving celebration and for the duration of Massasoit's life, relations between the colony and the Wampanaog were good.

IN THIS BAS-RELIEF,
OR SCULPTED WALL,
ON THE NATIONAL
MONUMENT AT
PLYMOUTH,
MASSACHUSETTS,
MASSASOIT AND THE
ENGLISH SIGN A
FRIENDSHIP TREATY.

After Massasoit died his son Wamsutta became *sachem*, or chief, of the Pokanoket village for a short time. Massasoit's younger son, Metacomet, was the next leader of the Wampanoag. Metacomet was known to the English settlers as King Philip.

By the time King Philip took over as leader of the Wampanoag, many more Europeans had arrived in New England and settled on land that belonged to various Indian tribes. In 1675, as tensions between the English and Indians grew, King Philip united the

IN 1675, METACOMET, OR KING PHILIP,
AND HIS GROUP OF INDIAN TRIBES
BATTLED THE ENGLISH COLONISTS.

HUNDREDS WERE KILLED IN KING PHILIP'S WAR,
INCLUDING KING PHILIP.

Wampanoag with other tribes in the area. The Indians attempted to drive the Europeans out in a struggle called King Philip's War.

At first King Philip's group of tribes had some success. However, the colonies of New England, Massachusetts, Rhode Island, and Connecticut formed a military alliance and eventually crushed the Wampanoag and their allies. Hundreds from both sides were killed, including King Philip and other Indian leaders. At the same time, smallpox was devastating the tribes. From the end of King Philip's War until today, the Wampanaog have struggled to maintain their identity as an American Indian tribe.

VILLAGES AND THEIR SACHEMS

The most important link in the structure of Wampanoag society was the family. Its size varied from season to season. In the winter as many as fifty members of one family built a large structure and lived together. In the warmer months the family split up and spent their time hunting, collecting plants, tending fields, fishing, and gathering shellfish. Sometimes, the families in a village might work together on larger jobs, like clearing new fields or building defenses.

Each Wampanoag village had a leader called a sachem. The position of sachem was usually passed from father to son. However, when a son took over from his father, he had to prove to the rest of the

A SACHEM WAS A PROMINENT LEADER WHO OFTEN
SPOKE FOR THE COMMUNITY. HERE, ONE SACHEM,
MASSASOIT, CONFERS WITH COLONISTS.

community that he was worthy of the honor or the community selected a new sachem. Sometimes, if a sachem did not have a son, a daughter became sachem. If a sachem did a really good job, then other sachems looked to him or her for leadership.

Europeans thought that sachems were like kings who had absolute rule and that alliances that were made with one sachem would be honored by other sachems. However, each village worked as an independent community with only loose ties to the other villages. Sachems could be replaced at any time. Even within a village the sachems did not rule alone. Each sachem consulted with a group of advisers before making decisions that would affect the community. This group of advisers was usually made up of the respected men of the community.

Successful sachems were supported by the people of their community. Each year the community had a celebration and gave gifts of food and other supplies to their sachem. The sachem would, in turn, give some of the extra gifts to families in need.

BELIEFS, CEREMONIES, AND LEGENDS

Today, as well as in the past, American Indians live in close harmony with their environment. The Wampanoag are no exception. They believe that Kiehtan is the creator of all things and that he has power over the universe. They pray to him for a bountiful harvest and thank him for their success. When giving thanks, the Wampanoag hold a celebration. During it they feast and dance. They also offer gifts.

The Wampanoag respect all living creatures. They kill only what they need and thank the spirit of the animal for giving up its life so that others might live.

The religious leaders of the Wampanoag were called powwaws. They made sure that proper religious

CEREMONIES MARKED SPECIAL EVENTS IN THE LIFE OF THE TRIBE.
WHEN A MEMBER OF THE COMMUNITY DIED, THE POWWAW, OR
RELIGIOUS LEADER, CONDUCTED THE BURIAL CEREMONY.

THE COLORFUL CLIFFS OF GAY HEAD, MASSACHUSETTS,
PROVIDE THE LOCAL PEOPLE WITH THE MATERIAL TO
CREATE REMARKABLE CLAY POTTERY.

practices were followed. They also provided remedies for curing the sick and led ceremonies for special events in the life of the tribe, such as planting, harvesting, hunting, marriage, births, deaths, and war. The Wampanoag also had formal ceremonies when a member of the community died. The Wampanoag buried their dead in common cemeteries. Often, personal belongings such as tools and weapons were buried with the body. The people believed that these items would be needed in the life beyond.

The Wampanoag had many legends. One tale tells of Maushop, the giant who lived on Martha's Vineyard, an island off Cape Cod. This giant befriended the Wampanoag. He was the creator of the islands off the present-day Massachusetts coast, including the cliffs of Gay Head, where the Wampanoag found different-colored clays for making pottery. It is said that the fog that frequently blankets the islands and Cape Cod is the smoke from Maushop's pipe. Finally, as the story goes, when the Europeans arrived, Maushop the giant left.

DAILY LIFE

Childhood and Education ➤ The family was the most important part of Wampanoag life. Each family took responsibility for the education and upbringing of its children. Before the birth of a baby, the soon-to-be father built a wooden cradleboard to hold the infant. A cradleboard was about 2 to 3 feet (60 to 90 cm) long and 1 foot (30 cm) wide. A mother could strap her baby into a cradleboard and carry it on her back. She could also hang the cradleboard from a nearby tree as she worked in the fields. This way mother and baby could keep in close contact.

Among the Wampanoag there was a division of labor among men and women. The men hunted and fished while the women usually tended the fields and gardens and did the cooking. When there were big jobs to do, the men and women worked together.

A CRADLEBOARD, LINED WITH FUR AND SUSPENDED
FROM A TREE, WAS COMFORTABLE FOR THE BABY AND
PRACTICAL FOR THE MOTHER.

Everyone, including the children, worked together during planting and harvesting time.

Adult family members educated their children by example. Wampanoag children did most of their learning by watching the adults. Although children were permitted to play, they also had much work to do. Young girls helped with the cooking while the boys helped the men gather wood, hunt, and harvest food from the forest or from the water.

When a boy neared manhood, his knowledge and abilities were tested. At the proper time, a boy's father or one of his uncles blindfolded him and led him far into the woods. If the boy was able to remain in the forest for a few months and returned home well fed and healthy, he was considered a man. To celebrate his passage from boyhood to manhood, the group held a feast. Shortly after this event, the young man would marry.

Wampanoag marriages were traditionally arranged. Young women had the right to leave their husbands if they turned out to be poor providers. Wives could also return to their own families if their husbands mistreated them. Men of power, such as the sachems, sometimes had more than one wife.

Farming and Gathering ➔ Farming was a vital part of Wampanoag life. They grew a variety of

SURVIVING ALONE IN THE WILDERNESS FOR A TIME
WAS A TEST OF MANHOOD FOR YOUNG BOYS.

crops. The most important of these was corn, which they planted in small hills about 3 feet (about 1 m) apart. In each hill, they planted three or four kernels of corn.

The Wampanoag also grew beans, squash, and pumpkins. Beans were planted with the corn. The summer vines of the beans climbed the cornstalks. The beans were ready before the corn matured.

The Wampanoag also grew a variety of squashes— pumpkins, crookneck, and acorn squash, to name a few. In addition to corn, beans, and squash, the Wampanoag also grew tobacco and gourds. Tobacco had ceremonial importance and was smoked and gourds were hollowed out and used as containers.

When clearing the fields, the Wampanoag cut down trees but left the stumps to hold the soil secure. Many American Indians also used controlled fires to clear land. Depending on the quality of the soil, after a number of years the fields would become "farmed out," or exhausted from too much farming, and the Wampanoag would have to clear new fields. Sometimes, whole villages moved to a new site. Most of the Wampanoag villages were along rivers and streams where there was fertile soil for growing crops.

The Green Corn Festival, one of the biggest Wampanoag thanksgiving celebrations, was held when

THE WAMPANOAG VALUED THEIR CORN CROPS
ABOVE ALL OTHERS.

the first corn and beans of the year were ripe. Corn and beans were picked and cooked fresh. Later, during the harvest season, the corn and beans were dried and stored for the long winter.

In addition to cultivated foods from the fields, the Wampanoag gathered many foods from the forest. In years of crop failure the harvest of foods from the forest might be all the Wampanoag would have to eat. In the spring and summer, there was a variety of fruit, including strawberries, currants, huckleberries, blueberries, grapes, raspberries, and cranberries. The Wampanoag ate these berries fresh and also dried and stored them for later use.

Wild onions and leeks also grew in the forest. In late summer, the Wampanoag dug up the roots of groundnut plants and stowed them away for winter, and in the fall they picked and stored acorns, chestnuts, and other nuts. The Jerusalem artichoke plant, a member of the sunflower family, was another source of food. The plant produces an enlarged, edible root called a tuber. Tubers are similar to potatoes. They can be either eaten raw or stored and cooked later.

Hunting ➜ In addition to harvesting the crops and gathering food from the wild, the Wampanoag hunted. Before the Europeans came to North America, game was plentiful and various. Wampanoag

FRUITS FOUND IN THE FOREST HAD SEVERAL USES: BLUE JUNIPER
BERRIES FOR MEDICINE, AND RED ROSE HIPS FOR TEA AND JELLY.

hunters depended particularly on the white-tailed deer for their survival.

Deer were not just a source of fresh meat. Every part of the deer was used. Deerskin was the primary material for clothing. Bones and antlers were used to make a variety of tools. The sinew, the strong material that connects muscle to bone, was used like string to tie things together.

After the harvest, a Wampanoag family might move to a hunting camp in the interior. At a hunting camp, the whole family helped with the work of butchering, drying meat, and tanning hides. Although a tribe might spend most of the year in a very small area, it claimed a large hunting ground.

The Wampanoag hunters used many different methods to hunt deer. Individual hunters stalked deer and shot them with a bow and arrow. At other times, they used snares to trap deer or held deer "drives."

For a deer drive, a large party of hunters formed a line in the woods. As the line of hunters advanced, they made as much noise as possible, driving the frightened deer in front of them. The fleeing deer were steered toward waiting hunters. They sometimes built fences in the shape of a large "V" in the woods, and the drivers would direct deer into the wide end of the "V." Other hunters waited at the narrow end,

HUNTERS TRACKED THEIR PREY AND
MADE GOOD USE OF ALL THEIR CATCH.

THIS SKETCH SHOWS A DEER DRIVE IN ACTION.

where they could easily spear the deer. This cooperative hunting was often very successful.

The Wampanoag also hunted or trapped a number of smaller animals, including raccoons and beavers. Rabbits were plentiful and could be shot with an arrow or snared. Huge flocks of waterfowl made their winter home in the marshes and bays of the Northeast. Geese, swans, and ducks were shot with arrows or trapped in nets. Turkeys, quail, and large woodland birds called grouse were plentiful in the nearby forests.

Fishing → In the months when game grew scarce, there was always plenty of fish. Even today, after hundreds of years of heavy fishing, the waters off southeastern Massachusetts and the coastal islands continue to have excellent fishing.

The Wampanoag fished all year. They fished in both fresh and salt water. In the summer, they fished from canoes on the ocean. In the winter, they lived inland and went ice fishing on rivers and ponds.

There were a number of techniques used to catch fish. The Wampanoag made hooks out of bone and

FISHING FROM A CANOE REQUIRED A SPEAR
WITH AN ATTACHED LINE.

attached them to lines. Spears and nets were also used. Fishing with line and hook went on all year. Another technique was the fish *weir*.

A fish weir is a series of walls or fences of sticks or stones placed in a bay or river. As the fish swim around the weir, they are forced into a narrow passage where they can be easily netted or speared. Weirs are especially effective during spring and fall spawning runs. They can be used over and over again.

In warm weather, the Wampanoag often set up camp by their fishing weirs. They dried some of their catch on racks left out in the sun, or over fires. Shellfish were also preserved in this way.

Clams, oysters, scallops, lobsters, and crabs were all part of the Wampanoag diet. Crabs were roasted in their shells, while other shellfish were skewered on sticks and then smoked. It was not unusual for the Wampanoag and other coastal tribes to catch lobsters that weighed more than 20 pounds (9 kg). Lobster was also used for bait.

Traditional Foods → The Wampanoag had a wide variety of foods to choose from and many ways to prepare them. The popular clambake originated among tribes of the Northeast. To prepare a clambake, they built a fire over rocks. When the rocks got

THE WAMPANOAG RELIED ON SEVERAL TOOLS TO CATCH FISH,
INCLUDING NETS, SPEARS, AND WEIRS.

CLAMS AND OTHER SHELLFISH APPEARED IN
MANY TRADITIONAL WAMPANOAG MEALS.

very hot, the coals were scraped away. The rocks were then covered with a layer of seaweed. Clams and other shellfish were placed on the seaweed along with fish and fresh corn. The food was then covered with a thick layer of seaweed. The top layer of seaweed retained the heat while the food cooked. Today, a clambake on the beach is still considered a special meal.

Fresh meat was boiled, broiled, roasted, or baked. To boil meat, it was added to water in vessels of wood, clay, or stone and placed over a fire. Broiling was done over hot coals. Roasting and baking was done in hot ashes. Stews were eaten all through the year. One kind of stew was called succotash. Its main ingredient was corn. Dried fish, meat,

DRYING IS ONE WAY TO PRESERVE FOOD. HERE, SLICES OF PUMPKIN HANG IN THE WARM SUN TO DRY.

squash, roots, and groundnuts were added to make it a hearty dish. Later, beans and other ingredients were added.

Corn was prepared in many different ways. The most common way was to grind it into meal and boil it with fish or meat. The next most popular way was to moisten the meal with water until it was the thickness of paste. This mixture would then be covered with leaves or corn husks, or made into little cakes, and then baked in hot ashes. This may have been the ancestor of today's "johnnycakes."

When Wampanoag hunters and warriors traveled, they carried another form of corn—dried corn kernels, which were parched over the fire and then ground up. This precooked ground corn could be eaten hot or cold with a little water added to it. A pack basket of this corn might last forty days. On short trips, the traveler carried enough in a belt pouch for a few days.

Corn was also made into a mush with currants or other berries and boiled. This was called samp. The tasty mixture was made into dumplings or flat cakes and was included in the diet of early colonists. Today, many of these recipes are still made.

Shelter ➔ Wampanoag shelters were called *weeto*, or wigwams by Europeans. They varied in size but were

AFTER THE FRESH CORN HAD DRIED, THE WOMEN GROUND
THE KERNELS WITH A GRINDING STONE AND PESTLE.

all built in the same manner. Long poles were driven into the ground and then bent over to meet a pole from the opposite side. The poles were then connected to one another with horizontal poles to give the walls strength. Once this framework was tied together, it was covered with bark and woven mats. A

THIS PLIMOUTH PLANTATION RECONSTRUCTION OF A WAMPANOAG BARK SHELTER WAS MADE ALMOST ENTIRELY OUT OF TREES.

THIS IS THE INTERIOR OF A WAMPANOAG WEETO THAT
WOULD HAVE BEEN USED DURING THE WINTER.

square smoke hole was left above the fire hole in the wigwam to allow smoke to escape. When the Wampanoag moved, they left the pole frame behind but took the mats with them.

In the summer, and at fishing or hunting camps, the average weeto was circular. It was about 15 feet (5 m) across and housed a single family. Winter weetos were much larger. They could be as wide as 30 feet (9 m) and as long as 100 feet (30 m). Inside the weeto there were a row of fires down the middle that burned to keep the interior warm. Mats woven of bulrushes or hemp—two types of tall, grassy plants that sometimes grow in marshes—were used for sleeping and sitting. Dried food supplies hung from the walls and ceiling. As many as fifty people might live together in one weeto.

Clothing ➔ The Wampanoag made their clothing out of the skins of moose, elk, and deer. The principle article of clothing for men and women—before the arrival of Europeans—was a deerskin breechcloth. It was a long piece of hide secured with a belt that hangs down from the waist in both the front and back. In the warm summer months, this clothing was all that the Wampanoag wore at home. The women also wore knee-length deerskin skirts.

A YOUNG WOMAN FROM PLIMOUTH PLANTATION WEARS
TRADITIONAL WAMPANOAG WINTER CLOTHING.

When the weather turned colder, or when traveling in the forest, the men wore deerskin leggings. These leggings went from the ankle to the top of the thigh. The women sometimes wore leggings, which covered only their calves.

A mantle, or a cape hung over one shoulder, was also worn. In the warm months, mantles of woven grass were worn to protect against insects. In the winter, fur mantles were worn for warmth. Some of the winter mantles were full length and reached the ground. In the coldest months of the year, an extra piece could be added to cover the exposed arm.

Belts were used to hold up the breechcloths and to keep the mantles in place. Snakeskins were sometimes used as belts. The Wampanoag often decorated their belts with fringe or with polished shell beads, called wampum. Wampum belts were considered a sign of wealth and became a kind of currency among the various American Indians of the Northeast. The Wampanoag wore pouches that hung from their belts to carry items such as food, tobacco, fire-starting materials, and other necessities.

Moccasins were made of moose hide because it was much stronger than deer hide. Moose, however, were not plentiful in their hunting areas, so most Wampanoag wore deerskin moccasins. Moccasins were made from a single piece of leather. The seam was

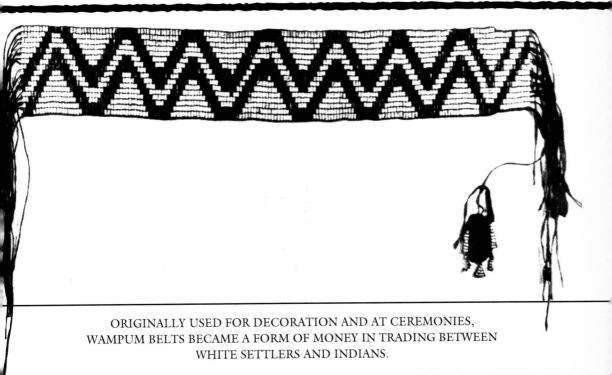

ORIGINALLY USED FOR DECORATION AND AT CEREMONIES,
WAMPUM BELTS BECAME A FORM OF MONEY IN TRADING BETWEEN
WHITE SETTLERS AND INDIANS.

covered with deer hide. Usually, plain moccasins were worn daily and decorated ones for special occasions.

Wampanoag women wore their long hair down, or in either braids or a ponytail. Some Wampanoag men wore their hair long while others wore theirs in a variety of styles. Eagle and turkey feathers were often used as decoration. Often people spent hours dressing their hair.

Traditional Wampanoag clothing was influenced by the Europeans who settled nearby. At first the Wampanoag used European textiles to make their usual garments. Eventually, however, they mixed the shirts, pants, and dresses of the colonists with their own traditional clothing.

Transportation → The Wampanoag had two ways to travel—walking or canoeing. There were established walking trails throughout the Northeast. Traces of these trails can still be found. Others have long since been wiped out by the roads and highways of modern times.

Their other form of transportation was the canoe. They built dugout canoes in a variety of sizes. Small dugouts carried one or two people while the largest canoes were 40 to 50 feet (12 to 15 m) long and could carry as many as forty people.

All dugout canoes were made in the same way. First, a suitable oak, chestnut, or pine tree was selected. Then, a fire was built around the base of the tree. When the fire had burned the tree, the charred wood was chipped away with stone axes. After the tree fell, the bark and limbs were removed.

Then it was time to burn out the inside of the tree to form the interior of the canoe. Wampanoag boatbuilders also used scrapers made from the thick shells of a type of local clam called quahog clams to

TWO DUGOUT CANOES, MADE FROM TREE TRUNKS, FLOAT IN THE WATER.

remove burned wood from the inside of the boat and to shape the outside. The ends were rounded with fire and an axe. In their dugout canoes, the Wampanoag traveled and fished all over the rivers, ponds, bays, and open ocean of their homeland.

THE WAMPANOAG TODAY

In a recent United States census, over 2,000 people identified themselves as Wampanoag. The majority of these people live in Massachusetts. Gay Head and Mashpee are the two primary communities. In each there are several hundred Wampanoag. Many of the other members of the Wampanoag tribe are spread throughout southeastern Massachusetts. One reason that the Wampanoag have not kept together as a single tribe is that they do not occupy one centralized reservation.

Starting in the 1950s, the Wampanoag organized classes to teach their young people their traditional language and culture. In the 1970s, the tribal government was reorganized in an attempt to unify the remaining Wampanoag.

TODAY'S WAMPANOAG HOLD ON TO THEIR PAST
AS THEY LOOK TO THE FUTURE.

A WAMPANOAG WOMAN CARRIES A PACK BASKET
OVER HER SHOULDERS AND CHEST. THESE
BASKETS OF STRAW ARE STILL MADE TODAY.

Some Wampanoag support themselves today, in part or entirely, through the production of traditional craft items. Baskets, beadwork, pottery, and other traditional crafts are sold at Plimouth Plantation in Plymouth, Massachusetts, and at various museums and reservations in the area.

Like many other tribes, the Wampanoag have had to fight for their rights in the courts. In 1987, the Wampanoag from Gay Head were finally federally recognized. The Wampanoag in Mashpee are currently appealing a case decided in 1979 in which the courts refused to recognize them. They presently have a petition filed for federal recognition.

The future of the Wampanoag will be determined by the attitude of the courts and the state and federal governments. It remains to be seen whether the U.S. government will fulfill their responsibilities to the people whose ancestors reached out a helping hand to the first Europeans who settled in New England more than three hundred years ago.

GLOSSARY

Algonquian language A language with several dialects spoken by many of the original peoples of the American Northeast and East.

Ice Age Also called the Pleistocene period, a time when a cooling of the climate worldwide caused vast glaciers to cover large regions of the earth, including much of North America.

Kiehtan The supreme being whom the Wampanoag believe created the world.

Maushop A legendary giant who lived on Martha's Vineyard and befriended the Wampanoag. He is said to have disappeared when the first Europeans arrived.

Nomadic Used to describe a people with no fixed residence, who move periodically usually in search of food and water.

Powwaw A Wampanoag religious leader.

Sachem The leader of a Wampanoag village. The position was usually passed from father to son. If a sachem had no son, the Wampanoag would sometimes choose a sachem's daughter to succeed him.

Weeto The Wampanoag name for their traditional dwellings.

Weir An obstacle built of nets, stones, or sticks that forces fish to swim through a narrow opening where they can be more easily caught.

Wigwam An Indian shelter with a frame of poles and hides. The word was adopted by Europeans to describe a variety of American Indian homes.

FOR FURTHER READING

Averill, Esther. *King Philip, the Indian Chief.* North Haven, Conn.: The Shoe String Press, 1993.

Bulla, Clyde R. *Squanto, Friend of the Pilgrims.* New York: Scholastic, 1990.

Peters, Russell M. *Clambake: A Wampanoag Tradition.* Minneapolis: Lerner Publications, 1992.

Siegel, Beatrice. *Indians of the Northeast Woodlands Before and After the Pilgrims.* New York: Walker and Company, 1992.

Weinstein-Farson, Laurie. *The Wampanoag.* New York: Chelsea House Publishers, 1989.

INDEX

ABOUT THE AUTHORS

Katherine Doherty is a librarian in a two-year college. Craig Doherty is an English teacher in a high school. With their daughter, Meghan, they lived on the Zuni Indian Reservation for five years, working in the Zuni Public School District. The Dohertys are also the authors of the Franklin Watts First Books *The Apaches and Navajos*, *The Iroquois*, *The Zunis*, and *The Penobscot*. They live in New Hampshire with their daughter.